Victorian Britain

VICTORIAN EDUCATION

Peter Hepplewhite

W

FRANKLIN WATTS
LONDON • SYDNEY

First published in 2009
by Franklin Watts

Franklin Watts
338 Euston Road
London NW1 3BH

Franklin Watts Australia
Level 17/207 Kent Street
Sydney, NSW 2000

Dewey classification number: 370.9

ISBN: 978 0 7496 8681 9

Planning and production by Discovery Books Limited
Editor: Helen Dwyer
Design: Simon Borrough

Printed in China

Franklin Watts is a division of Hachette Children's Books,
an Hachette UK company.
www.hachette.co.uk

Photo credits:
British Schools Museum, Hitchin: p. 11 both; Discovery Picture
Library: pp. 6, 7 right, 15, 26, 27 top, 29; Great Cressingham
School: p. 28; Peter Hepplewhite: pp. 7 left, 9, 10, 12, 13, 14, 19
bottom, 20, 21, 23 both, 25 both, 27 bottom; Mary Evans Picture
Library: pp. 4, 5, 8; Milton Keynes Museum: pp. 18, 19 top, 22;
www.picturesheffield.com: p. 16; www.picturethepast.org.uk: p.
24 (Courtesy of Magnus Church of England School)

CONTENTS

EDUCATING THE

❃

NATION

Queen Victoria was crowned in 1837 and reigned until her death in 1901. These years saw remarkable changes and, even before the Queen died, her people called themselves Victorians and spoke proudly of living through the Victorian Age.

By the 1850s, Britain had become the greatest industrial nation, with factories and workshops selling goods like fine cotton cloth and steam engines across the globe. At the same time the British navy controlled the seas, and the **British Empire** grew to include a quarter of the Earth's land and people.

Students and teachers in Eton College Court in the early 19th century wearing frock coats and top hats. At that time, many rich boys like these went to private schools like Eton, but very few poorer ones in England and Wales had the opportunity to go to any school.

A need for education

Yet, despite this success, there were underlying problems. By the 1860s, some of Britain's rivals, especially France and Prussia (now part of Germany), were catching up. One reason for this was that their people were better educated. The French and Prussian governments built schools, paid the teachers and told them what to teach. By comparison, British education was a hotchpotch.

Systems of education

Scotland was way ahead of England and Wales in education. In 1800, Scotland had local schools paid for by the **rates** in most towns and villages. In England and Wales most parents had to pay to send their children to school. The sons of wealthy families were sent to **public** (private) **schools** like Eton or Harrow, where they learnt mainly ancient history, Greek and Latin. By 1837, many ordinary children went to schools run by religious groups and charities. One of these was the National Society, set up by the Church of England. By 1851, there were 17,000 national schools with 956,000 pupils. The pupils were taught reading, writing and Bible stories, but little else.

Charities filled some of the gaps. From 1844, the Ragged School Union set up schools in **slum** areas of the new towns. Pupils were taught reading, writing and arithmetic, so they could find jobs and stay away from crime. But it was not until 1870 that the British government began to build and run schools, and it was 1880 before education became compulsory for children between five and ten years of age.

Robert Raikes and Sunday Schools

Robert Raikes (1736–1811) set up the first Sunday school in 1780 in Gloucester, at a time when most children did not go to school at all. He taught his pupils reading, Christianity and good manners. His idea was widely copied and by the time Victoria became queen 1.5 million children were attending Sunday schools.

A Sunday school in 1858. Notice some of the Ten Commandments from the Bible on the walls for the children to learn.

SCHOOLS FOR THE RICH

Most Victorian boys and girls could not go to school unless their parents could afford the fees. Children from some rich families were taught at home, at first by a **governess** then, when they were older, by private tutors (teachers).

Boys learned history, Latin and Greek. These subjects prepared them for university and a career, perhaps in the Church, law or politics. Girls were taught how to keep accounts, do embroidery (decorative sewing), to sing, play the piano and dance – subjects that would help them make good wives and manage their servants.

Public schools

More often boys from wealthy families were sent to live at public schools like Rugby, Eton, Harrow or Winchester by the time they were ten. In the early 19th century, these schools were harsh places with bad food and poor teaching. New boys became 'fags', or servants, to older boys, who bullied and often beat them.

Public School Riots
In 1818 in Eton school boys rioted and smashed their headmaster's desk. This hated headmaster was a 'champion flogger' who, even though he was 60 years old, found the energy to flog (beat) 80 boys in one day. In the same year, a riot at Winchester School had to be stopped with the help of two companies of foot soldiers with **bayonets**.

Boys at Rugby School in 1870 playing rugby. Private schools used sport to encourage team spirit and discipline, qualities boys would need in military careers. In 1880, one-fifth of all boys leaving Rugby and Harrow schools joined the armed services as officers.

In the 1830s, however, new headmasters like Thomas Arnold (1795-1842) of Rugby brought sweeping changes. Lessons were widened to include maths, geography and more recent history. Boys were taught to become 'Christian gentlemen' – religious, well-mannered and proud of their country. These improved public schools became very successful, with their pupils getting the best jobs in the country.

Grammar schools

Many **middle-class** families paid to send their boys to local **grammar schools**. There they learned subjects that would be useful to them when they started careers in business, industry or medicine. Lessons included arithmetic, languages and science.

Frances Mary Buss (1827–1894) opened the private North London Collegiate School for girls in 1850. The Girls' Public Day School Company was founded in 1872 to provide more affordable schooling for girls. By 1890, it had 34 schools teaching 6,504 middle-class girls. They were taught the same subjects as boys. Pupils from these schools went on to become the first women doctors and lawyers.

HOPEWELL HOUSE, NORTH ROAD,
HORSFORTH, NEAR LEEDS.

Mrs. HARTLEY'S SCHOOL
FOR YOUNG LADIES.

Terms per Quarter.

FOR TUITION IN ALL THE BRANCHES OF AN ENGLISH EDUCATION:

		£ s d
For Boarders above 12 Years of Age	... ...	£6 0 0
Ditto under 12 ditto	... ...	5 0 0
Weekly Boarders	... ...	4 0 0
For Day Pupils above 12 years of Age	... ...	1 1 0
Ditto under 12 ditto	... ...	0 15 0
Music	... ...	1 1 0
French	... ...	1 1 0
Drawing	... ...	0 10 6
Laundress	... ...	0 10 0
Single Dinners	... ...	0 0 6

Masters for French & Drilling.

Each Young Lady to be supplied with Slippers, Sheets, Pillow Cases, Towels, Toilet Soap, Fork and Spoon.
It is requested that each Day Pupil be provided with Slippers.

A Quarter's Notice required previous to the removal of a Pupil or a Quarter's payment.

(Above) This private girls' school in Horsforth, Yorkshire, charged the parents as much money for French or music lessons as it did for everything else put together.

Kendal Grammar School.

Head Master: Rev. GEORGE H. WILLIAMS, M.A.,
Late Scholar of Jesus College, Oxford; formerly Head Master of Kingsbridge Grammar School.

Second Master (Science): P. P. PLATT, B.A.,
Late Scholar of Corpus Christi College, Cambridge; 24th Senior Optime.

MATHEMATICS :—V. M. TURNBULL, M.A.,
Trinity College, Cambridge, 14th Wrangler.

GENERAL SUBJECTS & MODERN LANGUAGES :—
MONSIEUR LOUIS. R. I. HUGHES, B.A.,
Peterhouse, Cambridge.

Master of the Junior School: J. BROWN, B.A.,
Prizeman of Trinity College, Dublin; formerly Vice-Principal of Peterborough Training College.

MUSIC :—J. S. WINDER, Organist of St. Thomas', Kendal.

DRAWING :—G. H. DODGSON, Head Master of the Kendal School of Art.

SHORTHAND : T. GORDON-THOMPSON. DRILL : SERGEANT MIDGELEY.

SPLENDID Buildings on gravel soil. Mountain and Sea Air. New School House opened January, 1894, having accommodation for Thirty Boarders. Fives Court, Carpenter's Shop, Chemical Laboratory, &c., &c. Earnest preparation is offered at the hands of a strong Staff for Business, the Professions, and the Universities. Many rich Scholarships tenable at the School and at the University. Kendal is also one of the Northern Schools privileged to compete for the Hastings Exhibitions at Queen's College, Oxford, of the annual value of £90 for five

Like many other grammar schools, Kendal Grammar School could trace its history back to Tudor times but by 1894 it had modernised to teach subjects useful in an industrial age.

SCHOOLS FOR
THE POOR

At the start of the Victorian age, many children worked in fields, factories, mines or workshops and had little time to go to school. Even the few pennies they earned were an important part of the family income. Many adults, too – around 40 per cent – were unable to read or write.

A village dame school about 1840. The room is poorly furnished and crowded with children of widely different ages.

Dame schools

Parents who could afford a penny or two a week sent their children to dame schools. These were run in many villages by elderly men or women, often in their own homes. Some taught basic skills like reading and writing, while others were barely more than childminders. As one dame put it: 'It is not much they pay me and it is not much I teach them.'

Ragged schools

The idea of ragged schools was developed by John Pounds (1766–1839), a Portsmouth shoemaker. In 1818, he began teaching some of the poorest children in the town, without charging fees. Pounds inspired politician Lord Shaftesbury (1801–1885) to found the Ragged School Union in 1844. By 1861, there were 176 schools in the union.

Going to the Ragged School

For a long time crime caused by children has been a problem hence some friends of education in this town decided to set up a Ragged School. Within a few days nearly 40 boys were attending. To stop them returning to begging or stealing it was necessary to offer each child a pennyworth of bread and cheese daily.

First Report of the Newcastle upon Tyne Ragged School, 1848.

The first ragged school for boys in Newcastle upon Tyne was in Sandgate, one of the poorest areas of the city. This illustration shows a newer replacement school that was opened in 1855 in Jubilee Road, a more respectable part of the city. It had room for 140 boys and 60 girls to live there.

They were paid for by subscriptions from wealthy people who wanted poor people to have an education. Their pupils came from the worst slum areas and had a reputation for being dirty and unruly.

Factory and workhouse schools

In the towns and cities, some factory owners set up their own schools to educate their young workforce. Other bosses were forced to take action when new laws were passed in 1844 insisting that factory children should be given six half days' schooling every week. However, the teaching was often poor.

By the 1850s, every Victorian locality had a **workhouse** to offer basic care to families who had fallen on hard times. Many workhouses set up schools to teach the children to read and write so they could get jobs and not be poor themselves. One of the best workhouse schools was at Norwood, near London. This had the guns and mast of an old navy ship in its playground and it trained some boys for careers in the Royal Navy.

NATIONAL AND BRITISH
❋
SCHOOLS

Although most people in Victorian Britain thought of themselves as Christians, they did not all worship in the same way.

The biggest and most powerful faith group was the Church of England, or the Anglicans. The Queen was Head of the Anglican Church and its bishops sat in the House of Lords. Other Christian groups like the Methodists, Presbyterians and Baptists had broken away from the Church of England in the 1700s. They were called Dissenters, or Nonconformists.

Religious education

Both groups thought it was part of their Christian duty to try to educate poor children, especially if they learned religious ideas at the same time. The Nonconformists set up the British and Foreign Schools Society in 1808 and the Anglicans founded the National Society in 1811. Both groups were very good at raising money from powerful supporters to build schools. By 1870, the British and Foreign Society had about 300 schools in Wales alone and the National Society had over 1,000 in total.

Although parents paid a small fee to send their children to these schools, the schools had to be run as cheaply as possible to keep down costs. A single teacher could instruct a class of over 100 children with help of older pupils called **monitors**. The teacher taught the monitors, who then tried to teach groups

Skenfrith National School in Monmouthshire, Wales, was built in 1843. The datestone above the door celebrates its opening. By 1851, there were more than 17,000 national schools in England and Wales. Today the school is used as the village hall.

The British Schools Museum in Hitchin, Hertfordshire (top left), contains the only remaining monitorial schoolroom that was built to teach by the Lancasterian system (left). This system was the idea of Joseph Lancaster (1778–1838). One master taught 300 boys with the help of 30 monitors, who stood around the sides of the room. The boys used the desks and benches in the middle when they had to write.

of their younger schoolmates. When they had finished, the monitors went back to the teacher to find out what to do next.

Government help

The government slowly decided to help church and charity schools. From 1833, it offered a grant of £20,000 a year to be divided between all the schools. This was a tiny amount but important. As the grant went up, the government appointed **inspectors** to check standards and see that the money was being well spent.

BOARD SCHOOLS

❋

Despite the work of all these different schools, only around 60 per cent of children were in education in 1869. At least two million children, mostly in the slums of large industrial towns, were not at school at all. At last, a new Liberal government decided to take action.

The 1870 Education Act

In 1870, the government tried to push an Education Act through Parliament. This caused ferocious arguments because the Church of England did not want to see its power weakened and it campaigned against 'godless government schools'. In the end, a bargain was reached.

The 1870 Education Act said that school places must be available for all children between the ages of 5 and 10. To achieve this England and Wales were divided into about 2,500 schools districts, each with a school board. The boards were elected by **ratepayers** and it was the board's job to check if there were enough schools. If the churches, or other voluntary groups, could not provide schools, the boards could build schools to fill the missing places and pay for them out of the rates.

A race to build

A school-building campaign began with churches and school boards racing to provide places for children.

An extract from an 1874 Post Office Directory of London listing some of the Board Schools in Finsbury district. You can see from the staff names that many of the teachers were women.

LONDON SCHOOL BOARD.
33 New Bridge street E C.
Clerk, George Hector Croad, B.A
For Members of the Board, see 'OFFICIAL DIRECTORY.'

Finsbury (William Saunders, supt. of visitors), 36 Duncan terrace, City road **N**
— Allen st. Goswell road E C ; W. J. Plummer & Christopher Sibley, *masters ;* Emily L. Butt, Mary A. Tavener, Clara Edmonds & Helen C. Carter, *mistresses*
— Ann street, Wilmington square **WC** ; Miss Kate Rymer, *girls' mistress ;* Elizabeth C. Austen, *infants' mistress*
— Bath street, City road E C ; George J. Clarke, John James, George Drumgold & James Tucker, *masters ;* Elizabeth M. Sibly, Emily M. Holloway, *girls' mistresses ;* Victoria M. Smelt, Ellen Kendall, E. H. Strudwick, H. Pile & H. Yeates, *infants' mistresses*
— Blenheim road (iron building), Henry Lee & W. Kent, *masters*

Between 1870 and 1888, the number of children on school registers inspected by the government shot up from 1,152,000 to 4,688,000. By 1899, the school board in Sheffield, for example, had built or taken over 26 schools and was planning to build four more.

At first parents still had to pay fees. Attendance was voluntary and it was not until 1880 that going to school became compulsory. In 1891, education became free. The age at which children could leave school was raised to 11 in 1893 and 12 in 1899.

Simpson Street Board School in Sunderland is one of the few remaining board school buildings surviving from the 1880s. It is now rather run down and used as small workshops.

A Step Forward for Women

The 1870 Education Act gave women the right to vote for members of school boards at a time when they were not allowed to vote in other elections. Women were also allowed to serve on the school boards. In 1870, four women were elected including Elizabeth Garrett (1836–1917), a popular local doctor in Marylebone, London. She gained more votes than any other **candidate** in the country.

SCHOOL
✱
ARCHITECTURE

Victorian school buildings were a source of local pride. They were built to impress parents and children with the importance of learning. Most pupils lived in rows of crowded terraced houses near dirty factories, so architects tried to make up for their drab homes with uplifting and inspiring designs.

Grand styles

School sites were often quite small, so buildings had to be several storeys high to fit in all the rooms that were needed. In many areas, this made them the grandest public buildings around.

The most popular style of architecture was neo-Gothic, copying features from medieval buildings like cathedrals and churches. Neo-Gothic schools had

Ouseburn Board School in Newcastle upon Tyne was designed in 1893. The elaborate and very unusual style of the towers was based on a Burmese temple. Today it is used as a business centre.

New private schools could afford grand designs. This is an illustration of the newly built Reading Grammar School in 1871. It was designed by Alfred Waterhouse (1830–1905). He was an architect famous for neo-Gothic style buildings such as Manchester Town Hall and the Natural History Museum in London.

elaborate arched windows and doors, while roof lines might have spires or towers. Some school boards, especially in London, wanted something less religious-looking and went for the newer Queen Anne style. This led to picturesque buildings with features including tall **sash windows**, ornate chimneys, fancy **gable** ends and decoration with tiles or carvings.

School layout

Inside, the layout depended on the way children were taught. Early Victorian schools that used monitors had one or two huge rooms that could accommodate more than 100 children. Later schools with more trained teachers or pupil-teachers (see page 16) were built with a large central hall and classrooms leading off it. The headteacher would teach some lessons like games and music in the hall and be able to keep an eye on how the pupil-teachers were doing in the classrooms.

Newer schools had huge windows to let in as much light and fresh air as possible. If the school was large enough, infants and older boys and girls all had separate yards and entrances. Infants were taught on the first floor and the juniors on the second floor, in single-sex classes.

Where You Live

Do you have any Victorian schools near your home? Many are easy to identify because they are still used as schools, but others may now be used for other purposes like flats or businesses. They are usually built from dark-red bricks with windows set high in the walls to stop children looking out. Try to find a foundation stone with the date when the school was built. Look out for features like separate boys' and girls' yards or entrances.

AN ARMY OF
TEACHERS

Life was often hard for Victorian teachers. Many, especially in country schools, had no training, while others began their careers as pupil-teachers.

The three teachers and ten pupil teachers – aged about 14 – of St Mary's School in Walkley, Yorkshire, pose for a group photo.

Pupil-teachers

The system of pupil-teachers began in 1846 to replace the use of monitors. Boys and girls as young as 13 served a five-year **apprenticeship** in schools. They were paid around 3 shillings (15p) a week to help teach the different classes and were supervised by the headteacher and government inspectors. If they passed their exams they became qualified teachers when they were just 18.

on [crossed out] Monday or Mo

*Nov. 1   A little boy bit his sister on the arm,
very severely. I of course punished the boy.
I asked the girl to-day what her mother
said about the biting, and she said that
her mother thrashed her for telling 'hi'master'*

*Parents' attitudes to school could cause difficulties for teachers, as this page
from the 1878 log book of High Spen Board School in County Durham shows.*

Teachers needed

After 1870, an army of teachers had to be recruited to
staff all the new schools. In 1872, there were 37,714
teachers in inspected schools, but this number had
soared to 100,401 by 1888. Teaching soon became a way
for bright, **working-class** men and women to make
better lives for themselves. Women earned much less
than men but, despite this, teaching was one of the few
respectable occupations for women who wanted to be
independent. By 1888, women filled two-thirds of
teaching jobs, but the law said that they had to give up
their careers when they married.

School inspections

School inspections began in 1839 to make sure that
government money was being spent properly. Inspectors
checked school buildings and equipment, looked at the
timetable and the register and, most importantly of all,
tested the children. Teachers were not given their full
wages if the exam results were poor. Not surprisingly,
many teachers taught the children what they knew the
inspector was going to test. Lessons became very boring
as children learned the same things over and over again
until they knew everything off by heart.

Where You Live

You can find out what
life in a Victorian
school was like by
reading school log
books. They had to
be kept by all
headteachers after
1862 and are just like
a diary recording day-
to-day events.
Sometimes they
document ordinary
things like the weather,
absent teachers and
school visitors.
Sometimes events can
be very dramatic, like
outbreaks of diseases
or the deaths of
pupils. You can find
school log books in
your local record
offices – or there
might still be some
old log books in
your school.

VICTORIAN CLASSROOMS
AND EQUIPMENT

Modern school classrooms are bright, light and cheerful places with hi-tech equipment like computers and interactive whiteboards. Compared to these, many Victorian classrooms were plain and dull.

In country schools especially, conditions could be quite grim. The rooms would be heated by a single cast-iron stove or an open fire and were bitterly cold in winter. Several large classes might work noisily side by side, separated by nothing more than curtains.

*This Victorian classroom in Milton Keynes Museum shows many of the features of a Victorian classroom, including an iron stove for heating the room, an **abacus** for counting and stuffed birds for **object lessons**.*

Classes and classrooms

Bigger city schools had separate classrooms for each class, or 'standard'. Standards were introduced in 1862. Children older than seven were divided into six standards, like modern year-groups. They sat a test at the end of the year to see if they could pass into the next standard. If they didn't pass the test they had to stay with the younger children.

Pupils sat in rows of dark, varnished wooden desks, all facing the teacher's desk and the blackboard at the front. If boys and girls shared a room they sat on opposite sides, sometimes coming in and out of different doors. Often the teacher's desk was on a platform so that they could keep an eye out for bad behaviour.

Writing equipment

Equipment was quite basic. Paper was expensive so younger children wrote on slates with thin slate pencils. Their writing could be rubbed out with a damp cloth, or even a licked finger. Older pupils were allowed to use pens with nibs and ink. The ink was kept in large bottles and the ink monitors filled small china inkwells that fitted into holes on the desks. If they spilt the indelible ink on their fingers they could end up with skin stained blue for days.

Children practised writing from copy books, learning to shape letters very precisely. They had to be careful not to 'blot their copybooks'. Ink blots had to be carefully soaked up with sheets of absorbent blotting paper.

Handwriting Victorian Style

Would you like to learn to write like Victorian children did? You can still buy 'dippy pens' with nibs and bottles of ink quite cheaply and many museums sell reproduction slates and pencils. You can download examples from Victorian handwriting copy books from internet sites like Kirkleatham Museum in Redcar, Cleveland. Remember, in a Victorian classroom you would have to get each letter or number exactly right – or start again.

White china inkwells were carried in trays like this to pupils' desks. If they were too full, the ink was easy to spill.

VICTORIAN LESSONS

The most important lessons in Victorian schools were the three 'R's – Reading, wRiting and aRithmetic. Young children began reading and writing by learning the letters of the alphabet.

Reading and writing

When they knew the sounds they put them together to make simple words like 'talk', 'jump' and 'play'. Once they knew these off by heart, they were taught to add endings like 'ing' and 'ed' to make longer words like 'jumping' and 'jumped'.

Counting and measuring

Pupils often used an abacus to help them with their numeracy, moving the coloured beads to learn how to add and take away. Weights and measures were not in the simple metric system we use today. Instead of using counting systems based on tens, children had to learn complicated **imperial** measures.

'The Fusileer's Dog'

History meant learning a lot of dates, but also vivid poems and stories about the glories of British history. In Victorian times the Crimean War in the 1850s was the last big war Britain had fought in. Children would have loved the story of the brave army dog accidently killed by a cart:

Go, lift him gently from the wheels,
And soothe his dying pain,
For love and care e'en yet he feels,
Though love and care be vain.

'Tis sad that after all these years,
Our comrade and our friend,
The brave dog of the Fusileers,
Should meet with such an end.

Historical Ballads, *from which 'The Fusileer's Dog' is taken, was published in 1882 and featured poems about Britain's past, from the distant Roman period to the recent Crimean War.*

Imperial Weights and Lengths	
16 oz (16 ounces) = 1 lb (1 pound)	12 inches = 1 foot
14 lb = 1 stone	3 feet = 1 yard
2 stones = 1 quarter	1,760 yards = 1 mile
4 quarters = 1 hundredweight	
20 hundredweight = 1 ton	

Try adding together 1 yard 2 feet 8 inches and 3 yards 1 foot 7 inches!

Teaching methods

Basic science and technology were taught through object lessons. Objects included snails, frogs, crystals and minerals, seeds and shells and the work of blacksmiths and wheelwrights. Teachers often had object lesson kits that children could touch, or large posters they could look at. An object lesson was supposed to help children observe closely and discuss.

Victorian teaching methods could be quite boring. Pupils spent a long time learning things like tables in numeracy, lists of the dates of kings and queens in history or capital cities of the world in geography. This meant chanting them over and over again until they were word perfect – even if the children did not understand what they were learning. There was a lot of copying from the blackboard and writing down what the teacher was reading out loud.

This object lesson poster taught the children where milk came from and how butter was made.

DISCIPLINE AND

HEALTH

Victorian schools were very strict compared to those today. Teachers and most parents believed that children should learn to behave properly or they would become spoiled and learn bad ways.

School Rules
Every school had a set of rules covering behaviour, manners and neatness, for example:
- Behave respectfully and be lawful
- Be kind to others and never be rude
- Always speak the truth
- Keep the **Sabbath** [Sunday] holy
- Remain neat and tidy in appearance and care for all belongings.

Punishments
Victorian children were punished a lot and not just for breaking the rules. If they couldn't learn something properly, or forgot what they had learned, they could be punished for that too. Boys were caned across their bottoms and girls on their hands or the back of their legs. Many children were afraid of school because of this. Other punishments included a severe talking to, writing lines – copying the same sentence 50 or 100 times – or being made to wear a big hat with a capital D on it – the Dunce's Cap.

Sickness and disease
Most Victorian school children were actually lucky to be alive. In the 1880s,

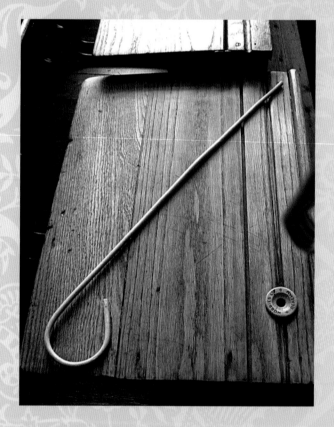

A typical Victorian teacher's cane. Caning replaced an earlier punishment called birching, in which children were beaten with a bunch of twigs tied together.

about one in every five children died before they were seven years old. Many came from very poor families, ate poor-quality food and lived in bad housing with no drains or clean water, where diseases spread quickly.

Scarlet Fever was considerably prevalent in the early part of the year, but had almost disappeared in the summer ; in the last seven months of the year only three deaths from the disease were recorded in the Borough. Since the opening of the new hospital I have been able to isolate such clamant cases of scarlet fever as became known to us.

Three deaths were ascribed to Diphtheria during the year.

Whooping Cough was the assigned cause of twenty deaths in 1883—a number under the average ; it seemed to have almost entirely disappeared from the town in the later months of the year.

Under the head of "Fever" are classed cases of Typhus, Typhoid, and Continued Fever. Two deaths were ascribed to Typhus during the year, from neither case was there any extension of the disease. Twelve deaths were attributed to Typhoid Fever, and one to Continued Fever.

Diarrhea.—35 deaths were due to this disease, 32 of these occurring in the months of July, August, September, and October

This extract from The Medical Officer of Health Report for South Shields in 1883 shows the seriousness of the main childhood diseases.

With lots of children gathering together, school could be a dangerous place. School log books are full of reports of outbreaks of measles, whooping cough, diphtheria, scarlet fever and typhoid. If one child had an infectious disease then it could spread quickly through the school and the nearby community. Often the local **Medical Officer of Health** had to close schools until outbreaks of fever had passed. Pupils and sometimes teachers died during these **epidemics.**

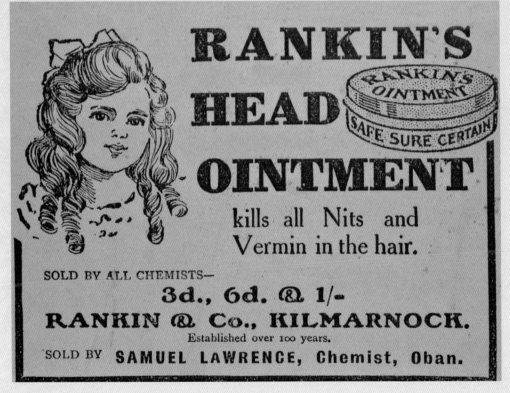

RANKIN'S HEAD OINTMENT

RANKIN'S OINTMENT

SAFE SURE CERTAIN

kills all Nits and Vermin in the hair.

SOLD BY ALL CHEMISTS—

3d., 6d. & 1/-

RANKIN & Co., KILMARNOCK.

Established over 100 years.

SOLD BY SAMUEL LAWRENCE, Chemist, Oban.

Most children caught head lice from others at school. They could be sent home if they were infested. As you may have found to your cost, head lice are still common today and remain very hard to treat.

GAMES, PRIZES ✤ AND TREATS

Boys at the Magnus Grammar School in Newark on Trent, Nottinghamshire, play leapfrog in the school yard.

Victorian schools could be fun, too, and children waited eagerly for break time. Boys' yards were often bigger than girls' because Victorians expected them to play rougher games like football and cricket, or 'battles' such as British soldiers against their enemies. Footballs didn't last long. They were often just a pig's bladder that was begged from a butcher and blown up to make a ball.

Teachers did not think girls needed as much space to run around. They played skipping and counting games or hopscotch. Some pastimes like blind man's buff, 'tag', rolling iron hoops or tiddlywinks were popular with both sexes.

Magic Lantern Shows

Magic lanterns were the Victorian equivalent of the digital projectors used in most classrooms today. Although the light came from an oil lamp, it cast a strong and clear beam to project sets of slides. The Victorians used magic lanterns for entertainment, education and moral teaching. Children's favourites were shows such as Wild Animals of the World or stories like *Aesop's Fables*.

Rewards

Victorians schools could be rewarding places. For good work, pupils could earn points or stars and at the end of the year those with the best results were given certificates or a prize, usually a book. Those few children who never missed school might be presented with a medal at assembly.

Getting out of school

Most teachers looked for ways to make lessons interesting. If something exciting was happening nearby, the children might be taken to have a look. It might be something hi-tech like a new steam traction engine operating at a farm or something awesome like battleships sailing past a seaside town.

School trips were common too, though usually pupils did not travel far. They might be taken to the park or the beach for a picnic or to the town museum to see a new exhibit. The children at Crickhowell British School in Powys did particularly well in 1875. They were taken on a pleasure boat outing on the Brecon and Abergavenny canal.

Special occasions usually meant treats. Schools commemorated Queen Victoria's Golden Jubilee in 1887 and her Diamond Jubilee in 1897. On both these national celebrations, children were given luxuries like special teas, bags of sweets, band concerts, souvenir mugs and extra holidays.

Books awarded to children for good work or attendance had prize certificates like this pasted into them. Can you read what this prize has been awarded for?

This magic lantern slide is taken from a show called 'Scrub, or the workhouse boy's first start in life', a best-selling Victorian children's book. Scrub is a workhouse boy who becomes a heroic servant, saving the life of the spoilt rich son of the family he works for.

EDUCATING ADULTS

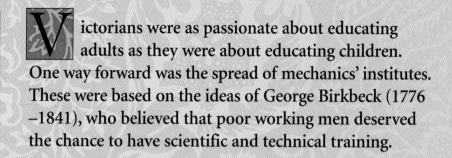

Victorians were as passionate about educating adults as they were about educating children. One way forward was the spread of mechanics' institutes. These were based on the ideas of George Birkbeck (1776 –1841), who believed that poor working men deserved the chance to have scientific and technical training.

Newspapers for Everyone

One of the greatest contributions to adult education was the boom in cheap newspapers. In 1846, there were 14 daily newspapers; by 1890 there were 180. The number of newsagents shops doubled in the 1880s alone.

Students at Trinity College, Cambridge, take exams in College Hall in 1842. They are sitting side by side and facing each other, so they can see what each other is writing!

Mechanics' institutes

The first institute was set up in Glasgow in 1821 and by 1840 there were 300 – one in almost every major town in Britain. Mechanics' institutes were paid for by membership fees or donations from rich supporters, often local **industrialists**. Facilities included libraries, conversation rooms, lecture theatres and collections of models, machines, minerals and specimens. Most classes were held at night or weekends when working men had time to study. Some institutes later became part of their local university. The London Mechanics' Institute for example was set up in 1823 and it became Birkbeck College in 1907 and part of London University in 1920.

Universities and colleges

Universities too faced startling changes. In 1800, there were only two universities in England – Oxford and Cambridge – and they were hopelessly old-fashioned. They were only open to men who were members of the Church of England and taught mainly Latin, Greek and theology (religion).

Female students attend a lecture at Girton College, near Cambridge, in 1877. The college was founded in 1873 to give women a university education. At first the college had only 15 students.

The Victorians founded a series of colleges in the large industrial towns like Manchester, Leeds, Liverpool and Newcastle. These colleges taught useful subjects like science and engineering and worked closely with local industries. From the 1870s, women began to demand entry to universities studying subjects such as art and medicine, although at first they were taught separately from men.

New skills

Increasing leisure time gave many ordinary men and women the chance to learn new skills through interests and hobbies. Choral singing was popular, most famously in Wales. By 1880, there were 4,000 brass bands in England with a national competition for the best bands held every year.

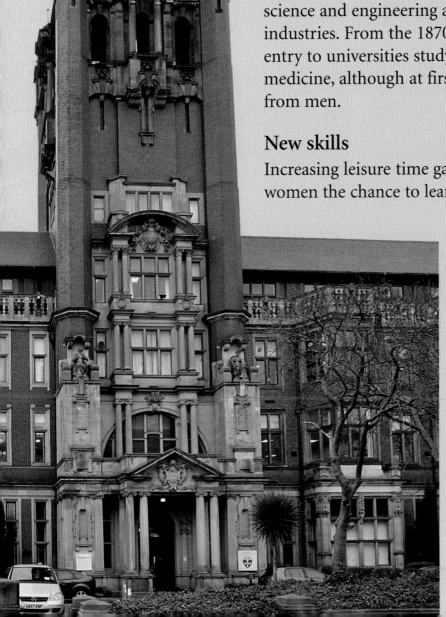

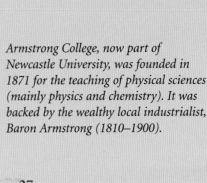

Armstrong College, now part of Newcastle University, was founded in 1871 for the teaching of physical sciences (mainly physics and chemistry). It was backed by the wealthy local industrialist, Baron Armstrong (1810–1900).

VICTORIAN LEGACY

❋

The Victorians are taught in history lessons in all primary schools today. One of the most popular field trips is to visit a museum that runs a Victorian schoolroom experience, where modern children are scolded by strict teachers who check their hands for cleanliness and make them chant tables or lists of old imperial measurements.

Great Cressingham School in Norfolk (left) was built in 1840. Today it invites children to step back in time, wear Victorian clothes and experience first-hand a day at a real Victorian school and try out Victorian games in the playground (below).

Books and films

Stories of Victorian schools come to us through books and films. Who can fail to squirm when the evil teacher, Wackford Squeers, beats poor Smike in Charles Dickens' novel *Nicholas Nickleby*? Or even worse, when plucky Tom is tortured by Flashman in Thomas Hughes' *Tom Brown's School Days*?

Victorian Schools in Danger

In 2004, the government announced a huge school building and modernisation programme spending £36 billion by 2020. Every secondary school and half of all primary schools will be given state-of-the art facilities. But the danger is that, in the excitement of spending all this money, many sturdy old schools that have survived for more than 100 years will be demolished because it is often cheaper to knock them down and start again rather than refurbish them.

Run by government

If you go to school today, you can't escape the Victorian legacy. In some ways their ideas still affect the way you are taught. The government pays for and tightly controls most education. Government inspectors still come in to check teaching standards and, although it's a last resort, they can close schools they think are failing. On the other hand, successful schools attract more pupils and get more government money – a form of payment by results. Children are still tested regularly, and some people still complain that too much teaching is aimed at passing the test, not real learning.

Happier schools

In other ways however, schools have changed a lot. Teachers are no longer allowed to hit and humiliate children to keep them under control. They usually try to make lessons fun, encourage children to find out what they are good at and help them learn at their own pace. Classrooms are bright, cheerful places with tables that move for different activities, not just fixed rows of desks for formal lessons.

Bonner Street Primary School in Hackney, one of the early London board schools, was demolished in 2006 even though there was a lively local campaign to save it and there was nothing wrong with the building itself.

GLOSSARY

❊

abacus a tool for making calculations by sliding counters along rods.

apprenticeship a training course for a job.

bayonet a knife attached to the end of a rifle.

British Empire all the countries around the world ruled by Britain.

candidate someone who puts themself forward to be elected.

epidemic when an infectious disease that is easily passed from person to person affects many people at the same time.

gable the triangular end of a building where the roof slopes meet.

governess a woman employed to teach children in their own home.

grammar school a (usually) fee-paying school for well-off boys.

imperial describes traditional measurements used in Britain before the metric system was introduced.

industrialist a business person who built up a large industry.

inspector a person appointed to inspect schools to make sure the children are being taught correctly.

Medical Officer of Health a doctor in charge of local health care.

middle-class describes people with some wealth, like doctors and lawyers.

monitor an older pupil put in charge of teaching younger pupils.

object lesson a lesson in which an object is used to explain an idea.

public school fee paying schools for richer people.

rates local property taxes, paid by householders and businesses.

ratepayer a person who paid a local property tax to the council and the school board in Victorian times.

Sabbath Sunday, the traditional Christian day of rest and worship.

sash window a style of window frame that slides up and down.

slum housing unfit for human habitation.

workhouse an unpleasant refuge where the very poor lived if they had no money.

working-class describes most ordinary people who worked in hard, lower paid jobs, like miners and factory workers.

TIMELINE

❊

1808 Nonconformists found the British and Foreign Schools Society to set up British Schools.

1811 Anglicans found the National Society to set up National Schools.

1821 First mechanics' institute is set up in Glasgow.

1833 Government grants £20,000 to charity schools.

1837 Victoria becomes queen.

1839 Government appoints inspectors to check standards in church schools.

1844 Lord Shaftesbury founds the Ragged School Union for poor children.

1850 Frances Mary Buss opens the North London Collegiate College School for girls.

1862 All head teachers must now keep school log books.

1870 Education Act says that all children aged 5 to 10 should go to school and establishes board schools.

1872 Girls' Public Day School Trust is founded.

1880 Attendance at elementary school becomes compulsory for all children between the ages of 5 and 10.

1891 Elementary education becomes free.

1893 School-leaving age raised to 11.

1899 School-leaving age raised to 12.

1901 Queen Victoria dies.

PLACES TO VISIT

❋

British Schools Museum,
Hitchin, Hertfordshire
http://home.btconnect.com/
hitchinbritishschools
Tells the story of elementary
education from 1810 until
1969 and includes a galleried
classroom built in 1853.

**Great Cressingham Victorian
School**, Norfolk http://
www.victorianschool.com
Experience a day at a real
Victorian school, built in
1840, heated by a coal-fired
stove and lit by an oil lamp.

Milton Keynes Museum
http://www.mkmuseum.org.
uk/exhibit/school.htm
In the Victorian Schoolroom
visitors can look through old
text books or see examples of
work created by children in
Victorian times.

Ragged School Museum,
London http://
www.raggedschool
museum.org.uk/nextgen
Once a ragged school, this
museum offers roleplay,
hands-on exhibits and talks.

**Scotland Street Museum of
Education**, Glasgow http://
www.glasgowmuseums.com/v
enue/index.cfm?venueid=12
Find out about the public
school and the history of
education in Scotland through
displays, audio-visuals and
restored classrooms.

WEBSITES

❋

**http://history.powys.org.uk/
school1/education/edmenu.
shtml**
The history of education in
mid-Wales from photographs,
documents, maps and
museum exhibits. 'Victorian
Powys' for schools looks at the
changes that took place in 18
small towns.

http://www.victorians.org.uk
Virtual Victorians website
from Tiverton Museum. It
explores the themes of
childhood and education
through artefacts and
pictures.

**http://www.channel4.com/
history/microsites/Q/qca/
victorians**
Channel 4's Victorian
Children microsite. Discover
what life was like for children
living in Victorian Britain.

**http://www.bbc.co.uk/schools
/victorians/index.shtml**
Find out about children in
Victorian Britain in 'History
for Kids' on the BBC website.

INDEX